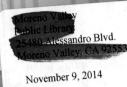

FUN
FIERCE FISH!

20 FUN FACTS ABOUT
PIRANHAS

MVFOL

By Heather Moore Niver

Gareth Stevens
Publishing
Moreno Valley Public Library

Please visit our website, www.garethstevens.com. For a free color catalog of all our high-quality books, call toll free 1-800-542-2595 or fax 1-877-542-2596.

Library of Congress Cataloging-in-Publication Data

Niver, Heather Moore.
20 fun facts about piranhas / Heather Moore Niver.
    p. cm. — (Fun fact file: fierce fish!)
Includes index.
ISBN 978-1-4339-6988-1 (pbk.)
ISBN 978-1-4339-6989-8 (6-pack)
ISBN 978-1-4339-6987-4 (library binding)
1. Piranhas—Juvenile literature. I. Title. II. Title: Twenty fun facts about piranhas.
QL638.C5N58 2012
597'.48—dc23

2011050928

First Edition

Published in 2013 by
Gareth Stevens Publishing
111 East 14th Street, Suite 349
New York, NY 10003

Copyright © 2013 Gareth Stevens Publishing

Designer: Ben Gardner
Editor: Greg Roza

Photo credits: Cover, p. 1 Dmitrijs Mihejevs/Shutterstock.com; p. 5 Photofish/Shutterstock.com; p. 6 SimonG/Shutterstock.com; p. 7 guentermanaus/Shutterstock.com; p. 8 Maxim Tupikov/Shutterstock.com; p. 9 iStockphoto.com/Anna Bryukhanova; p. 10 Janne Hämäläinen/Shutterstock.com; p. 11 fstockfoto/Shutterstock.com; p. 12 Tina Rencelj/Shutterstock.com; p. 13 Rodger Jackman/Oxford Scientific/Getty Images; p. 14 Juha Sompinmäki/Shutterstock.com; pp. 15, 18 Morales/age fotostock/Getty Images; p. 16 Panache Productions/Oxford Scientific/Getty Images; p. 17 Herbert Eisengruber/Shutterstock.com; p. 20 l i g h t p o e t/Shutterstock.com; p. 21 iStockphoto.com/Sterling Stevens; p. 22 iStockphoto.com/ricardoazoury; p. 23 Yellowj/Shutterstock.com; p. 24 DEA / C. DANI/De Agostini Picture Library/Getty Images; p. 25 iStockphoto.com/Brasil2; p. 26 iStockphoto.com/tomch; p. 27 Jacques Jangoux/Photo Researchers/Getty Images; p. 29 Sergey Kartashov/Shutterstock.com.

Printed in the United States of America

CPSIA compliance information: Batch #CS12GS: For further information contact Gareth Stevens, New York, New York at 1-800-542-2595.

Contents

Words in the glossary appear in **bold** type the first time they are used in the text.

Presenting Piranhas

If any fish is known for being mean and nasty, it's the piranha. Piranhas have small but sharp teeth, and many kinds have a taste for blood. The red-bellied piranha can be rather nasty. It helps give all piranhas a fierce **reputation**.

A scary movie from 1978 called *Piranha* helped give this fish a bad name. But they aren't always the cruel killers movies and stories make them out to be. Many of them aren't **aggressive**. Some even eat plants and seeds instead of flesh.

Terribly Toothy!

FACT 1

Piranhas have razor-sharp teeth.

There are more than 60 **species** of piranhas. They're all part of the Characidae (kuh-RAA-sih-dye) family, which also includes pet fish such as the colorful tetra. Most piranhas have large, rounded heads and short, narrow bodies. They're best known for their razor-sharp teeth and strong jaws.

A piranha's jaws are so strong they can chomp right through bone or even a steel fishhook. Ouch!

A piranha's teeth are triangle shaped. When the fish closes its mouth, the top and bottom teeth fit tightly together like scissors.

FACT 2

The word "piranha" means "tooth fish."

Piranhas get their name from a Brazilian Indian language called Tupi. The Tupi word *pirah* means "fish," and *ranha* means "tooth." The piranha's teeth are only about 0.16 inch (4 mm) long, but they sure are sharp.

FACT 3

Piranhas can grow to be 2 feet (61 cm) long.

Most piranhas are between about 8 and 12 inches (20.3 and 30.5 cm) long. The largest can grow to about 2 feet (61 cm) long.

Most are silver with red patches. Some are so dark they look black.

Some piranhas have silver scales that sparkle in the light.

Common Piranhas

name	largest size
black spot piranha	11 inches (28 cm)
lobe-toothed piranha	7.9 inches (20 cm)
pirambeba	7.9 inches (20 cm)
redeye piranha	16 inches (41 cm)
red piranha	19.7 inches (50 cm)
San Francisco piranha	13.4 inches (34 cm)
slender piranha	11.8 inches (30 cm)
speckled piranha	8.3 inches (21 cm)
white piranha	8.3 inches (21 cm)
wimple piranha	6 inches (15 cm)

FACT 4

Piranhas are native only to freshwater in South America.

Piranhas live in every country in South America. They live in freshwater sources from northern Argentina up to Colombia. Most kinds of piranhas live in the Amazon River, where 20 different species like to swim.

Orinoco River

Many piranha species live in the Orinoco River in Venezuela.

FACT 5

Some piranhas have "escaped" South America to live in other areas.

Recently, piranhas have been found as far north as the United States, even in the Potomac River. People may have put their pet piranhas in the river. However, water so far north gets too cold for them to survive for long.

FACT 6

Most piranhas swim and hunt in fast-moving water.

Piranhas live together in schools called shoals. Shoals spend a lot of time in freshwater rivers and streams where the current moves quickly. Of course, they like it best if there's lots of **prey** there for them to hunt.

Piranha Prey and Other Snacks

The piranha menu has many different choices.

Piranhas rarely chow down on humans or animals that are bigger than they are. Piranhas are **omnivores** that eat fruit and seeds along with other fish. Some munch on birds, snakes, and small **mammals**. They often eat **carrion**.

Piranhas are drawn to the smell of blood, but most of the time they eat whatever they can find.

cherimoya fruit

FACT 8

Some piranhas help plant new trees.

Some piranhas are **herbivores**. In the Amazon River, piranhas eat the seeds of sweetsop, soursop, and cherimoya (chehr-uh-MOY-uh) trees. The fish carefully eat the seeds and leave them in another place. This helps new trees grow in other areas.

Feeding Frenzy!

Piranhas often work in groups to eat their prey—while it's still alive.

Many scary piranha stories come from one way they gobble their meals. When a shoal of piranhas smells blood, they rush to the source and chow down. This is called a feeding frenzy. The hungry fish will start eating an animal while it's still alive!

Feeding frenzies aren't common. Most of the time, frenzies start when there isn't enough food around for all the piranhas.

A piranha feeding frenzy can make the water "boil."

Feeding frenzies often last just a few minutes. After one fish takes a bite, it moves to the side so another can get in for a nibble. Piranhas move so much and eat so fast it sometimes looks like the water is boiling.

Piranhas can smell blood from 100 feet (30.5 m) away.

Most shoals include about 20 fish. But hundreds of piranhas may eat during a feeding frenzy.

FACT 11

A feeding frenzy can get so crazy that the piranhas take bites out of each other.

A piranha doesn't stop to chew its food. When the fish bites down, the food goes straight into its stomach. It keeps eating until its belly is full. With many piranhas all eating at the same time, they often bite each other by mistake!

FACT 12

Piranhas can pull a whole cow into the water.

Piranhas can grab a very weak cow by the nose while it's drinking and pull it into the water. But not many eat that way. Wimple piranhas nip bits out of the scales and fins of passing fish. These fish can grow the bitten parts back.

Red-bellied piranhas feed quickly on a duck that has recently died.

Piranha Diets

young
fruits

plants

young **crustaceans**

adults
fins and flesh of other fish

weak cattle

young birds

lizards

sea crabs

mammals

small fish

their own young

pets
fresh or frozen fish similar to what they would eat in the wild

vegetables

FACT 13

US president Theodore Roosevelt watched a cow get eaten by piranhas!

In 1913, US president Theodore Roosevelt was on a hunting trip in Brazil. While he stood at the edge of the Amazon River, he saw a shoal of piranhas eat every scrap of meat off a cow skeleton. What a scary sight!

Stories say that the local Brazilians wanted to put on a show for Roosevelt. So they filled part of the river with hungry piranhas before feeding the cow to them.

Don't misjudge these little guys. Red-bellied piranhas are small but dangerous.

The red-bellied piranha is one of the smallest and meanest piranhas of them all.

Red-bellied piranhas are among the smallest piranha species. They weigh only about 3 pounds (1.4 kg). However, they're also widely believed to be the most aggressive species of piranha. Black piranhas are the next nastiest.

Predators Are Prey

Even tough fish like piranhas have to watch their backs.

Piranhas may be some of the fiercest fish in world, but they have **predators**, too. Crocodiles, Amazon River dolphins called botos, and herons enjoy a juicy piranha for dinner. Given the chance, turtles and larger fish will gulp down a piranha as well.

This alligator has caught a piranha for lunch.

FACT 16

Piranhas swim in shoals to scare off predators.

Scientists used to think that piranhas only swam in very large shoals so they could hunt better. But they actually swim this way for safety reasons. Predators, such as dolphins, are less likely to strike when there are lots of piranhas around.

Fishy Family

FACT 17

Piranha moms and dads both take care of their eggs.

In April or May, a pair of male and female piranhas will make a nest. The female lays about 5,000 eggs at a time. Mom and dad do such a great job of protecting their eggs that almost 90 percent of them hatch.

Piranha eggs hatch after just a few days.

People and Piranhas

Piranha teeth can be made into useful tools.

Some South Americans catch piranhas just for their teeth. Those knife-like teeth can be made into handy tools and

weapons. However, piranhas can be trouble for fishermen. They steal the fishermen's bait, harm nets, and of course sometimes bite the fishermen.

People hunt piranhas for food and to keep as pets.

25

Even the red-bellied piranha can be kept in a fish tank, as long as it's not against the law in your area.

FACT 19

Keeping a piranha as a pet may be against the law.

In some places, it's against the law to own a pet piranha.

But a few kinds of piranhas can be kept as pets in other areas.

They're unhappy if they don't have lots of plants and dark places

to hide. Watch your fingers!

FACT 20

Increased piranha attacks may be caused by human activities.

People have built dams on the Amazon River, slowing down the water. Piranhas prefer to lay eggs in calm waters. People like these waters for swimming. So, people and piranhas are meeting up more often than ever before.

This is the Tucuruí Dam on the Amazon River in Brazil.

Fast Food Fans

Piranhas don't usually kill people, but they're one kind of fish to avoid when you're out for a swim. For such a little fish, the piranha sure can do some harm. However, some of them prefer to eat veggies.

Old stories say that a shoal of piranhas could eat every last scrap of a cow in less than a minute. That may be a tall tale. But piranhas have definitely figured out how to get food fast!

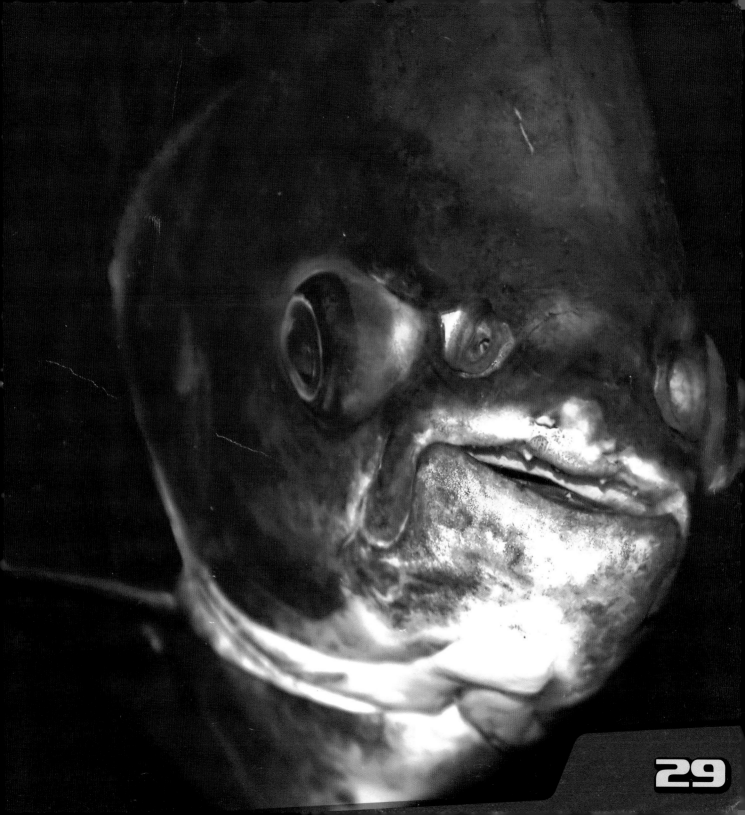

29

Glossary

aggressive: mean or likely to attack

carrion: a dead, rotting animal

crustacean: an animal with a hard shell, jointed limbs, feelers, and no backbone

herbivore: an animal that only eats plants

mammal: a warm-blooded animal that has a backbone and hair, breathes air, and feeds milk to its young

omnivore: an animal that eats both meat and plants

predator: an animal that hunts other animals for food

prey: an animal hunted by other animals for food

reputation: the common beliefs that people generally have about someone or something

species: a group of living things that are all of the same kind

weapon: something used to fight off an enemy

For More Information

Books

Berendes, Mary. *Piranhas*. Mankato, MN: Child's World, 2008.

Coldiron, Deborah. *Piranhas*. Edina, MN: ABDO, 2009.

Storad, Conrad J. *Piranhas*. Minneapolis, MN: Lerner Publications, 2009.

Websites

Amazing Piranha Fish
www.worldmostamazingthings.com/2011/05/piranha-fish-amazing-piranha-facts.html
Learn more about the piranha with a diagram and great photos!

Can piranhas really strip a cow to the bone in under a minute?
animals.howstuffworks.com/animal-facts/piranha-eat-cows.htm
Discover more about piranhas with news, facts, and photos.

Index